Civil War

Experiences

of a

German Emigrant

Company D,
12th Michigan Regiment

By

1st Lt. Joseph Ruff

Editor: Dorothy May Mercer

ISBN 13: 978-1-62329-090-0
ISBN 10: 1-62329-090-2

Cover picture:
The Civil War. The battle of Shiloh. Chromolithograph by
Thulstrup de Thure, 1888. By Everett Collection
Licensed by shutterstock.com

This is a non-fiction account of the first year of the Civil War.
Most of the material is either licensed (as above) or is now edited
and re-published with permission from the original publishers. (See
credits elsewhere.) The editorial remarks are original.

"...As I took cover behind a tree, hardly large enough to cover me, and kept busily firing, several enemy bullets were driven into the tree about at the line of my head. One just clipped by my right ear..."

"We were endeavoring to carry off our wounded, and so our progress was slow. As soon as that movement began, the enemy followed, pouring a galling fire upon us." Pg 23

"The day closed with the Union army still holding sufficient ground to stand. I stayed in the line until I lost every comrade of my company." Pg 24

'By two o'clock, the Confederates gave up the struggle and began their retreat back to Corinth. ... We followed up the retreating army and found, among the fallen, Blue and Gray intermingled. Some were cold and stark in the embrace of death, some were breathing out their lives. Thousands of them had lain there all night, torn and bleeding, with no hand to lend assistance." Pg 25

"...as I tramped over the battlefield, thick with darkness and occasional rain, I stumbled over something, and, bending down to see more distinctly, I found myself looking into the face of a dead soldier." Pg. 27

"... He who cares for all His children must surely have been watching over me." Pg. 29

"We made a lively hustle over the fence, and, while I was getting over it, a cannonball struck the panel of fence from under me."

"At this point, there was a short bend in the river, and, there, those troops were unmercifully cut to pieces."

"I remember seeing by the bridge an oak tree, partly hollow, into which a little black boy had crowded himself all shivering with fright. There he crouched in terror, while the bullets tore the bark from the tree and made the slivers fly." Pg 39

Original Title:

CIVIL WAR EXPERIENCES OF A GERMAN EMIGRANT
AS TOLD BY THE LATE JOSEPH RUFF OF ALBION

Reprinted by permission from MICHIGAN HISTORY
MAGAZINE, Vol XXVII, Spring 1943 And MICHIGAN
HISTORY MAGAZINE, Vol XXVII, Summer 1943

1ST Lt. Joseph Ruff (1841-1921)

A native of Germany, he came to America as a child in 1851. Ruff served as a sergeant, and later lieutenant in the 12th Michigan Infantry. The badge he is wearing states "Company D 12 Michigan."

TABLE OF CONTENTS

CIVIL WAR EXPERIENCES of a GERMAN EMIGRANT,
Company D, 12th Michigan Regiment

Chapter One

How I Got Here

BEFORE beginning to write up the experiences of my military life, I wish to tell some of the things which happened to me before the Civil War. These will explain in part how I came to enter upon so important a period of our national life. I gained my first impressions of the political life of this great country the same year that I worked on the farm when I first came to Michigan. That was in 1856, the presidential year. I remember it; three parties were in the field. The Republicans nominated John C. Fremont for their standard bearer, the Democrats, James Buchanan, and the American, or Know-Nothing Party, Millard Fillmore. The latter had in its platform the peculiar principle that no foreigner should obtain citizenship until after a residence of twenty-one years, claiming that according to the Constitution no native-born could receive the electoral franchise in a shorter tine, and therefore it should not be given to foreigners any sooner.

The campaign of 1856 was a heated one. My employer was a Republican, and I naturally adopted his ideals and principles. I came, later, to feel, as I learned more and more about them that they harmonized best with my own ideas of what political principles should be, and I have never changed that view. One of the proudest acts of my political life was when I voted for Mr. Lincoln for second term. I, frequently, heard the slavery question discussed, often with blows, and my sympathies were drawn out towards the distracted colored people. I think, about this time or soon afterward, I read *Uncle Tom's Cabin* and the debates of Mr. Douglas and Mr. Lincoln, in 1858. There were several Democrats in the neighborhood with whom my employer used to discuss the political situation. So heated did they become in reciting their personal grievances that, often, they nearly came to blows.

In telling this I am trying to give a background for my later entrance into the war. That was a result of many personal experiences, one of which, at least, was one of the severe tests of my life. I had settled my people in Michigan, procured for them a shelter to live in, and started them with a chance in life. After that, I went to work on a farm for the man who owned the house my parents lived in. It was a large farm of 600 acres, usually hiring two men. I hired out for ten dollars a month in the winter and twelve dollars in the summer.

It was in the fall of the year that I got my people from Buffalo to Michigan, and, by that time, it was past the crop season. There was nothing more to grow for maintenance. My people looked to me for help, and for that first year much of my wages went to them. I bought them a cow, got them chickens and pigs, and labored early and late for two long years. I could only supply myself with bare necessities, and, at the end of the second year, I concluded to quit. It was late in the season, and I had been cleaning out the barnyard. It was getting cold. My garments were thin, my toes began to appear through my shoes, and I had not known what it was to have underwear or an overcoat. My mother made my mittens out of old bags. Winter was at the door.

As I soon learned to read and write in the English language, I became very much interested in reading about the national affairs of that day. I was much interested in American history, especially the Revolutionary War. The sacrifice and suffering of those who struggled to bring civil and religious liberty and make this great America an independent nation began to grip me with patriotic feeling. Among the several books I read in my spare time was a book called *The Impending Crisis* written by a man named Helper. The book set forth the conditions of the two sections, North and South, Slave States and Free States. The report was statistical and treated every phase of political, social, commercial, religious, and moral life and showed the progress of every industry under free labor and under slave labor.

War Clouds Threaten

All this was in the winter of 1860-61, and the war clouds were already threatening. Already South Carolina had passed her "Ordinance of Secession," the *Star of the West* had been fired upon out of Charleston Harbor, the South had refused to allow the government to provision Fort Sumpter, and everyone awaited in breathless suspense for the torch to be applied that would let loose the dogs of war.

So the winter passed. I was getting all the knowledge I could obtain that would give me an understanding of the part I was to take in the great conflict. I was in good health and enjoyed my work. On the first of April, when my term of service was up, I hired out again on a farm at thirteen dollars a month. It was shortly after that news flashed across the country that Fort Sumter had been fired on and that the President had called for 75,000 volunteers to suppress this rebellion.

No one can know, who did not pass through it, the breathless waiting and watching of the days that followed, but all that has been told by abler men than I am. My mind was made up as to what I would do if the conflict should continue. Of course I had hired out for the season and promised to stay with my employer, but as soon as my time was out, I determined to join myself to the Union Army. When the first real clash took place at Bull Run and resulted so disastrously to the Union arms, I could scarcely contain myself from starting at once. As the summer passed, each new report from the army confirmed my resolve to enlist. My people were now more able to take care of themselves as others in the family came to be older and could work.

Enlistment

As soon as my time was up, I could not rest or settle myself until I had placed my signature on the enlistment roll. I planned to set out one nice, warm, sunshiny day, the 16th of December 1861. After dinner, I got ready. I had nerved myself up for the ordeal of parting and feared to loiter lest I should fail. I remember well how I stepped to the door and stood, knob in hand, ready to go. I said to mother, as I opened the door, that I was going to Albion and that she was not to worry if I did not return that night. I knew full well how she would feel, as she mistrusted what I was intending to do. I could not endure to see her break down, and so I went quickly. How many mothers had to pass through that trial in the four years that followed!

I walked the eight miles to Albion, impelled every mile by the desire to help in my humble way in the saving of this great nation. Arriving at my destination, I proceeded at once to the recruiting office of Capt. Graves, and, as soon as I intimated that I was intending to enlist, he urged me to subscribe my name on the enlistment roll. He told me I would make a fine soldier and declared that I would be wearing the shoulder straps in three months. How far he came from his prophesy, this story will tell. After inquiring as to the regiment, company, and organization I was to join, I placed my name on the enlistment roll: Description: five feet, nine inches high, brown hair and eyes, age twenty, enlisted Dec. 16, 1861. The captain directed me to make my headquarters at the hotel.

The next day was a fine, pleasant one, and the captain called upon me in the evening, saying there was a squad to go out to camp at Niles, Michigan. "The porter of the hotel will call you at midnight," he said. I was called at the appointed hour and went out on the street. Several others were there to go, but there was no martial band to send us off with music, flags, and cheers. We marched over to the railroad depot. The train soon arrived. No demonstration—not a soul—to say, "God bless you, hope you will come back."

We boarded the train and were whirled away, not knowing what was before us. We reached Niles about sunrise and marched the remaining two miles to the campground. A guard pacing across the main entrance ordered us to halt. We were afraid he might enforce the command by firing his little, short popgun at us, so we stopped. While the Corporal of the guard was coming, we noticed a number of raw recruits standing inside rubbering their necks off to see who and what we were. Presently, one of them broke out calling "Fresh fish." The "fresh fish" were ordered to advance, which we did, mixing up with the other raw "fish," and, while we were talking with some with whom we were acquainted, a cowbell rang. The initiated bunch started to run like so many horses and left us wondering what

it was all about. They yelled back to us to come on and have "grub."
It was breakfast time, and we also broke into a run.

The rushing column turned into a long-board shed, where long
tables were set with bread, meat, and coffee. We "fell to" like hungry
wolves. In a few moments, the tables were bare. We had partaken
for the first time of Uncle Sam's bounty.

Guard Duty and Drill

After a little time, while we were getting acquainted with some
of the advanced recruits, the drums beat and those who were detailed
for guard duty began to assemble. These guards were detailed for
twenty-four hours and were on two hours and off four. Each change
required time. A Sergeant had charge of the entire guard. Guard duty
was one of the first things required of a new recruit. Next, came the
drill hour. Recruits were divided into squads until the companies
were organized. The facings, rankings in files, right or left in
column, four ranks and flanking, the wheeling (which was a difficult
movement), and finally the battalion drill with the entire regiment,
all came in due course.

But now, to go back, the next day, Dec. 19, the mustering officer
came to muster all eligible recruits into the United States Service.
He placed himself in front of the column, and, as each man's name
was called, the recruit stepped out four paces in front. We had all
been previously examined by an army surgeon, and only those
who were up to requirements were placed in line for muster.
Those who were accepted were told to uncover (still remaining in
line) and raise the right hand to Heaven, while the Iron-clad Oath was
administered. That oath confirmed us as subjects and soldiers of the
United States Service from the 19th day of December 1861 for eight
years or during the war, and when we dropped our hands and
recovered our heads, we were no longer our own but belonged to the
United States. We had agreed to be governed by the U.S. Army
regulations and to obey the President of the United States and all
officers placed over us. We were signed and sealed for duty
whenever and wherever called.

It is not necessary to mention all the details of our training. The sick calls, guard duty, maneuvering, calls for drill, and fatigue duty were parts of the day's routine. It had been quite pleasant weather, ever since we came. We were quartered in the buildings on a Fair Ground, not very warm or substantial, but they served. Each company had its own kitchen and dining hall provided with long tables, but no seats. There were no uniforms provided until into the New Year.

Christmas Furlough

Christmas Day was a fine day, and I remember most of the boys had a celebration of some kind. Somehow or other, there was a Christmas dinner for Company D in which fowls, of one kind and another, figured largely. Of course, these provisions were not ordered by Uncle Sam! About this time, I received a furlough for five days to visit my home. My people were glad to see me, and the days were all too short.

Arriving once more in camp, our soldier life commenced in dead earnest. I was placed on camp guard, and on Sunday I went on post about eight o'clock. It began to snow, and before my two hours were up, I was wading ankle deep. The winter had come. Of course, our quarters were provided with stoves, and wood was furnished, but, nevertheless, we suffered severely with the cold.

Our beds consisted of boards (no springs or mattress) with a little loose straw, and, for a considerable time, with insufficient blankets for covering.

The camp had its guard house where, now and then, some refractory recruit would be placed under guard, perhaps for breaking out of camp without permission. In which case, he was picked up by the provost guard and found usually to be, more or less, "tuned up" with firewater. In January, the uniforms began to come, all made alike and of army blue. As far as fit was concerned, the thinner the soldier, the looser was his cloth—l ike a coat on a bean pole—somewhat different from our World War soldiers!

Gradually, we began to be supplied with all the war materials to prepare an infantry regiment for the field; that is, accoutrements, knapsacks, haversacks, canteens, and (a little later) guns, bayonets, belts, and cartridges. After that, we were drilled in the Manual of Arms. Our guns were the Austrian rifles—poor guns made on the spur of the moment. It was a hard matter to sight and then make any sure execution when firing in battle line, but usually the bullet hit somewhere!

As additional recruits kept coming in, the companies were filled, and another muster took place on January 8th. A full quota of officers was supplied: field officers, colonel, and lieut. colonel, major, surgeon and assistant surgeons, quartermaster, and adjutant. Of course, as the regiment began to be filled up, there also appeared with its numbers of sick, the army hospital. There was no building in the camp suitable, and so a residence building was secured about five blocks down into the city.

Sicknesses of various kinds soon attacked the new recruits. That was the soldier's great enemy. The first man in our company to succumb did so as a result of taking cold during an attack of measles. I doubt whether he had proper care. His father came for the body. I and another comrade were retained as guard of honor until he was received into the train and interred in the family cemetery. Not long after this, I myself took an awfully bad cold and had considerable fever and a cankered sore throat. I remained in camp and was obliged to report sick and to proceed to the hospital to receive my medicine and have my throat treated. I thought the treatment a cruel one. I could not see that it did me much good, after a whole week of sore throat, to have a coarse brush saturated with some kind of solution poked down me. I asked the doctor how often I had to come to take that kind of treatment.

He was a Swiss-German, a little, dried-up old man with not much sympathy for our soldiers. After the Battle of Shiloh, he cared more for the enemy's soldiers than for us. He swore at me and said I might be pleased if I should get well in two or three weeks. I went once or twice, but an experience like that usually tried the metal of a soldier and made him think of home and mother.

As the regiment was rapidly filling up, and we had received uniforms, arms, and accoutrements, we trained in battalion drill and dress parade in which we made quite a show for the people of Niles. They always came out to see us, especially on Sunday afternoons.

7

The 22nd of February was a memorable day for the regiment. We were drawn up in line and marched out of camp into an open field where we formed a hollow square. A double sleigh soon appeared, drawn by two spirited, black horses, and carrying a number of ladies from Niles.

Halting in the middle of the hollow square, one of the ladies rose up in the sleigh and displayed a beautiful silk flag, which she presented in a few well-chosen remarks, to the colonel, Frances Quinn, who in turn accepted it for the regiment.

This flag was sewn by hand by the ladies of Niles and bore the inscription "Michigan expects every man to do his duty." This flag was borne by the regiment for the first two years of service. The color sergeant was wounded at Shiloh and afterwards died.

Some years ago I had a photograph taken of the flag, showing its tattered folds. By a general order from U. S. Grant, after the Battle of Middleburg, Tennessee, this flag was to have all the battles engaged in, up to that time, inscribed on its folds.

After the return south of the regiment from re-enlistment and furlough, a new set of colors were given us by the State and the old Niles flag was retained by Col. W. H. Graves of Adrian, Michigan. He kept it until his death; and then, it was turned over to his brother, S. E. Graves, in whose care, I believe, it is still kept.

Monotony

As time passed in our daily duties, preparing for the active field of war, camp life began to be monotonous, and many were the speculations that went the camp around as to what disposition would be made of us when finally ready. There was considerable anxiety to be in the front, doing something. And yet not a few began to get cold feet! It was beginning to dawn on them that a soldier's life was not made up of picnics and frolics, and that we had not yet arrived on the field of battle nor undergone many of the privations and sufferings of war with sickness and death, always ahead. These things were yet to come, and we began to think again of home and mother.

Some complained and even wished themselves out of it, as of this class there are always some. They grumbled and found fault continuously. Where could have been their patriotism, or what could they have been expecting—to be feted and feasted? It had been made evident that if we saved the Nation from destruction, it would be a long pull, a strong pull, and a pull altogether.

Orders to Move

About the middle of February, there went a rumor through the camp that we would receive orders to move. The regiment was now fairly well equipped. With Spring on its way when operations could commence in the South, most of us were anxious to be in the field. The final order came, at last, about the 15th of March, and all was bustle getting ready. Letters were written, and some of the superfluous articles which could not be carried in our knapsacks were sent home.

March 19, 1862, Leaving

On the 19th of March, we started out for St. Louis. The line of march, from the camp to the railroad depot, was a sight to see. The air was chilly and filled with fine snow. Yet on the march, the sun broke through the clouds, at times presenting an inspiring sight—a sea of slashing bayonets, the colors flying and the bands playing. All the city of Niles had turned out to see us off, as well as a big crowd of people from all the surrounding country. Many of them had relatives and friends in that column stepping to the music.

Just the day before, I had graduated into manhood's age—twenty-one years.

At the depot, the loading commenced at once. There were four freight cars for the officers' horses and the quartermaster's stores and twenty-four passenger cars for the human freight. The sad reflection that, in all probability, many of us would never return was, in a measure, forgotten in boarding the cars and arranging ourselves with our swelled knapsacks, haversacks, canteens, and guns. The cars used in that day were not like the modern cars, nor like the Pullmans that carried our overseas soldiers. At last, we were loaded, and the train began to move amidst the cheers of the crowds, the waving of flags, the goodbyes, and God-bless-yous.

In that mass of people, might be seen fathers, mothers, brothers, and sisters and sweethearts, with tearful eyes, wondering whether they would have the joy of beholding their loved ones. This same experience was being exacted almost every day all over this great land.

Our first stop was made at Buchanan where a large crowd assembled. Here the same scenes were repeated, for many of the men had friends among the people gathered there.

One thing I shall never forget: Out of the crowd stepped a man bearing a basket of the finest, nicest friedcakes. Stepping up into the car he first began to pass them out so that all might get a share of the good cheer he was bearing in that basket. But the train began to move and so, also, had our benefactor. Lifting his basket above our heads, he poured out his wonderful gifts, first on one side of the car and then on the other. No time was lost among us of getting our share, while, amidst cheers and shouts, the man sprang safely to the ground. This one incident, I am sure, all have remembered. It relieved the tension of parting feelings

All through our service, through the exposure and hardships that try men's souls, there were always a few characters among so many who with a witty and ready tongue could bring out something to relieve tension and discouragement. This was one of the things which kept us from getting morbid and thinking of the home we had left far behind.

I had never come this way before, and, as the train sped on its way through villages and open country, my mind was constantly occupied with the passing scenery. It kept me, as well as others, from thinking too much of home and friends. In every village and even out in the open country, whenever it was noticed, as we passed that it was soldiers being sped forward to the front, flags and handkerchiefs were waving

Calumet

Arriving at Calumet, (now South Chicago), our train was switched on the Chicago and Alton railroad and, soon, was speeding its way across the Illinois prairies. At Joliet or Peoria, Illinois, the train stopped to give us coffee and let us eat our lunch. The crowded condition in which we found ourselves was beginning to be tedious. To lie down was impossible. It was difficult even to turn around. On through the night, the train kept speeding, stopping only for water or coal or to let another train pass on a sidetrack. I think the train was drawn by two locomotives. By daylight, we were passing through Springfield, the home of our illustrious President, Abraham Lincoln. Finally, about ten o'clock we arrived at Alton on the Mississippi River and disembarked from the train. It was surely a great relief for, having been confined twenty-four hours in such cramped and crowded conditions, our feet had really become numb.

Mississippi Steamer

A steamer was lying in wait for us in the river. We boarded, and, after all was loaded, we swung out on the breast of the Father of Rivers. This also was a new experience to most of us, and twenty-five miles down this river brought us up to the wharf at St. Louis. There we disembarked and were drawn up in line along the wharf. With our accoutrements and knapsacks, we stood in line for two whole hours waiting for General H. W. Halleck to make up his mind when and where to send us. We had not had any breakfast and stood wondering if he cared.

After some discussion, we were marched on board a large river steamer, for the present. We made ourselves as comfortable as we could in the crowded and cramped conditions. With the chill of a northeast wind upon us, we tried to crowd ourselves into the engine room to keep warm. But never mind, boys! We've answered our country's call, so brace up, for there's more still ahead.

Next day a steamer came up the river loaded with Confederate prisoners from Fort Donelson, and a sorry-looking lot they were, shivering with cold and but thinly clad for a northern climate. We felt sorry for them but did not know how soon some of us would have to change places with them. Our fears were fulfilled in the near future. That same day, after the prisoners were unloaded, we were changed over to their steamer. Here an incident occurred which showed what a "greenie" a raw recruit is.

On the steamer we first boarded were stacks of hardtack boxes. We had heard a great deal about soldiers eating hardtack, and, so eager were some of the soldiers, that a guard had to be placed to keep them from breaking into the boxes, so that they might sample Uncle Sam's dainties. They finally succeeded in doing it, too. While in the training camp at Niles, we had received baker's bread, baked and brought into camp by some contractor. Also, before starting, each man received three days' rations of soft bread. But so eager were these soldiers when they succeeded in breaking into the boxes of hardtack, that in order to make way for it in their haversacks, they took out the soft bread and threw it into the river. Some were more cautious. They got some, first, and sampled it, and, of course, not finding it so very palatable, they were wise enough to retain their soft bread as long as it lasted, satisfied that it would be time enough for the other when we could get nothing else.

Heading Downriver

The third day after arriving at St. Louis, our steamer backed out from the wharf and headed down stream with the precious human freight. While the higher officers may have known our destination, so far as the common soldier is concerned, he is not expected to know from one move to another what is before him. His is not to ask the reason why; his is but to do and die. The weather was, yet, quite chilly, and it snowed some while we were at St. Louis.

I do not know how to describe our condition on that steamer. If you have never seen one of those river steamers, you can not imagine how one thousand men could find room to make themselves comfortable from the cold in chilly weather. Of course, the officers occupied the cabin rooms, and some place for sick was provided. But the privates had to be content with such things as were possible, and that was certainly not bandbox style! The second day, we arrived at Cairo, Illinois, the point where the Ohio River flows into the Mississippi. Here, we noticed for the first time a little war-like preparation. On the point of land extending out between the two rivers, forts had been erected to command the rivers, and troops were stationed. A stop was made here, and General B. M. Prentiss boarded the steamer with his staff to take command of a division in Grant's army at Pittsburg Landing on the West Bank of the Tennessee River to which our regiment was assigned.

Paducah, Kentucky

That same afternoon, our steamer moved up the Ohio River and landed at Paducah, Kentucky, at the mouth of the Tennessee River. The Ohio River was a swirling flood overflowing its banks far out on the flats on the Kentucky side. All kinds of flood furniture were floating in the stream: chicken coops, hog pens, and portions of buildings. It was a sight to behold!

We laid up again on the crowded boat to spend the night. We had no cooked food. The only warm thing was coffee which each soldier prepared for himself. Each put the coffee beans in the bottom of his tin cup and, after crushing it with his bayonet, held it under the scalding water from the steam pipe. We were six days and night on that steamer, and the only cheer we got was what we made ourselves when someone would start up "John Brown's Body Lies Moldering in the Grave" and at the other end "We'll Hang Jeff Davis on a Sour Apple Tree." Such diversion relieved us from trying conditions. Our steamer (the Luminary it was called) lay up at the mouth of the Tennessee during the night. Some of our Company D quartered upon the hurricane deck on account of the crowded condition below. There was no shelter over our heads, only the blue of a star-lit sky.

Incident

An incident occurred here which might have been serious; yet, in another way it caused considerable amusement. Just across the river, on the Illinois side, was a camp of Illinois infantry. After it became full daylight, we, up on the hurricane deck, were watching their movements. The sergeant had stepped in front of the company tents for roll call. Half a dozen came out in line, and he began calling the roll. Pretty soon, some more crawled out of their tents. As the first had already answered all the names, up to that time, they, now, exchanged places with the newcomers and crawled back into their tents. So it kept on until all had attended the roll call. It was very amusing for us to see such unmilitary proceedings.

We had noticed, meanwhile, a black boy down near the river. He seemed to be carrying something in his hand, but we paid little attention, being more interested in the roll call. Suddenly a bullet came whizzing across, passed between the legs of one of our boys who was sitting on the cabin deck and struck through the cabin window, where it sent pieces of glass all over the table where the officers were eating their breakfast. There was an instant's bustle around that table. Probably, everyone thought we had been attacked.

Presently, out from the front end of the cabin, down the stairs to the lower deck, and out from the gang plank, came the officer of the guard inquiring what this was all about. He was a great tall redheaded Irishman and, I guess, was red enough otherwise by that time!

The black boy was pointed out to him as the cause of the disturbance. Starting after that boy in double-quick time, he caught him by the neck, jerked him up into the air, and basted him where he sat down until he yelled.

"You black spalpeen of a N------r," he cried. "I'll learn you not to be shooting this careless way." Of course, by this time the whole regiment had rushed out to see what was going on.

Some years ago at a reunion, I asked the question in open session whether any comrade present could tell when the 12th Michigan Infantry was first fired upon and where. Not a word was heard. Lieutenant Flanigan being present, I called out, "Oh, Lieutenant. Flanigan, do you remember where you basted that little boy for firing his pistol, and where the bullet hit?"

And, sure enough, he remembered.

Passed Fort Henry and Savannah

During the next forenoon, we passed Fort Henry where a Confederate force had fortified themselves. Quite a naval battle occurred there, later, and the fort was captured by Gen. Grant's army. From now on, up the river, we began to be more watchful. I think a gunboat went ahead of us. The weather began to be warmer, and as we passed Savannah we knew we were getting near our destination.

Pittsburg Landing

Along in the morning of the sixth day, we stopped near Pittsburg Landing. Here were several steamers unloading; and so, our steamer had to go a little distance above. The whole regiment (all accoutered) disembarked. Climbing up the steep bluff from the river, we marched the little distance to the Landing. Here was all military bustle. Camps appeared in the timber back from the river. We halted in an open field where our first camp was staked out by Lieut. Col. W. H. Graves. He had been in the service three months and understood how it was done. Long before night, the entire regiment was quartered for the first time under canvas, in the enemy's country the 26th day of March, 1862—just ten days before the battle.

Chapter Two

Battling Begins

Battling began, in fact, almost at once. While there were none of us killed, our enemies were getting our blood up. It was a long fight, and a strong fight, and a fight altogether. I think none escaped the fighting, neither high nor low, neither rich nor poor.

Settling In

As soon as we were settled, we took the first opportunity we had to get out our knapsacks for a change of underwear and clean shirts. On removing our underwear and our shirts, we found to our horror that we were covered with those nasty, crawling, gripping, graybacks who were feasting on our loyal blood. We immediately went on a war of extermination, and a long war we had! We got them from being jammed and crowded in that dirty, old steamer that brought up the Fort Donelson prisoners. We just got seeded down with them, and they must have liked our Yankee blood. It is not a pleasant subject. Nevertheless, all fared alike, no soldier escaped, and, while the graybacks were a constant menace to us, yet they occasioned considerable merriment throughout all our service.

The area, now Shiloh military park, as purchased by the United States Government, was soon covered with the white tents of the Union Army. Of course, we, now, had to be initiated into all the conditions of military life in the active field. Picket and guard duty, drill and fatigue duties, and new conditions regarding cooking and eating. All that, we gradually adjusted to. Cooking was a problem for the new recruits, for cooking in camp "kittles" over an open fire sometimes cooks the food, but far oftener, simply burns it. But it was a case of eating your feast of beans, pork, and hardtack with your tin plate and cup of coffee, sitting on a log or on the ground, on your lap, and begin. Of course, all of these things were improved in time, as we got initiated by hard experience.

Most everyone has heard of how the Union soldier could adjust himself to all kinds of weather. We were given severe tests under trial conditions and took advantage of every opportunity, afforded, to improve our powers of endurance amid the exposures of camp and field. A few days after we arrived, we shifted our camp, marched about three miles, and took up the front and centerline of our army, where we joined General Prentiss' division. We pitched our tents and again resumed our camp life. Our camp was located in the timber on a very pleasant piece of ground near a spring that afforded us good water. Those who were off duty broke the monotony of camp life, somewhat, by interesting reading, and writing to friends, while a good portion passed their time playing cards.

Unforgettable Sunday Service

The last Sunday before the battle, a chaplain from an Ohio regiment from Sherman's division, at the request of our chaplain, Eldred, came to hold divine service. The bugle call was announced and those who were interested, or drawn there, gathered and sat in a circle on the ground. A couple of hardtack boxes had been secured for a pulpit upon which was placed a somewhat dim light. Here, indeed, was a scene for an artist. A familiar hymn or two were sung, after which the chaplain led in prayer. To me this was a very solemn and impressive service and one which I never forgot.

The man of God seemed to be deeply touched, and some high spiritual feeling seemed to inspire him, while a feeling of awe crept over the rest of us. This certainly was in deep contrast to the time, just a week from that very hour, when over some thirty-six-hundred acres of battlefield, thousands of brave men lay silent in death, while numbers, untold, were bleeding and dying, and hundreds of wounded were being moved to the rear. Then the place was to resound with the crack of musketry, the roar of heavy artillery from the gunboats, and mingled groans and shouts of victor and vanquished. What a change from that Sabbath evening's hour of divine service!

Chapter Three—Battle of Shiloh

Grant vs Halleck

In speaking of the battle itself, I do not wish to go into it historically for that has already been done. Nor do I want to go into detail. Much has been written in regard to it; and yet, there are points which are not yet understood. I do not know if they ever will be. General Grant says in his *Memoirs,* "No battle of the Civil War is so misunderstood as the Battle of Shiloh, and sometimes I think purposely so." Now, what did General Grant mean when he said that? It is generally understood that General Grant was, at that time, under orders from General H. W. Halleck with headquarters at St. Louis, Missouri. Grant could act only according to Halleck's orders, and anyone who has read about it or who was in active service at that time knows the circumstances and feelings existing between these two men after Grant's victory at Fort Donelson. They can readily understand the position of General Grant at the time he was restored to his command at Pittsburg. He was under orders from Halleck, and although the army was his to command, he was to hold his forces until the arrival of General Buell who was coming from Nashville, Tennessee with 25,000 men to join Grant. Then the combined army was to move on to Corinth, Mississippi where the Confederate army was concentrating 42,000 men. The only order of General Halleck was the above order. There was no order for Grant to fortify himself for his own defense in view of the possibility that the Confederate army might come out of Corinth, only twenty-two miles away, and give battle before General Buell's forces would arrive.

Near Disaster

This is just what the Confederates did, and the result came close to a disastrous defeat. The fortifying could have been easily accomplished; inasmuch as, in flank and rear, we were naturally fortified. Positions in front could have been selected in which we could easily have fortified ourselves in a short time.

It is now many years since that terrible conflict, and most of the actors in it have gone to their reward. It is not my purpose to present any comment for argument but just to note a few points about the movements of both armies. Why the Union army should have been resting so quietly without taking the usual military precautions in front of an enemy, I believe I have already hinted at in the status of feeling between department commander and the active commander of the army. I have been very much interested in the study of that campaign and have drawn from the reports of both armies, and also from officials in high rank in the Confederate army.

Confederate Plans

As soon as it was ascertained at Confederate headquarters at Corinth that General Buell had left Nashville with 25,000 men, plans were set on foot, at once. Scouts were immediately put on his trail and reported to Corinth every night. The distance from Nashville was 125 miles, and they could readily figure approximately when he would reach Pittsburg to make a junction with Grant. And so, the head generals of the Confederates planned that, if they could move out upon Grant's army, combat it singly, and secure his surrender, it would then be an easy matter to secure Buell's army when it arrived.

This the Confederates resolved to do, and the world knows they did. I do not think it is generally sensed what the results might easily have been if the Confederate plans had succeeded more fully. With the combined Union army either captured or annihilated, what was to hinder the Confederate army from recovering Tennessee and Kentucky and, even, crossing the Ohio into the North?

But there is an old saying, and is it not the truth, that "man proposes but God disposes?"

Some may not agree with me on the point I wish to make here, but at any rate, let us go to Corinth, now, where the Confederate army is encamped.

The plans have been made to move upon the Union army at Pittsburg Landing. By a conference of their commanding generals, after midnight on the second of April, orders were given out to every commanding general of a division that the move is to commence at high noon on the third of April. The routes, assignments in the line of march, and orders to the flanking divisions to concentrate at a little hamlet called Monterey, nine miles distant, have been perfectly understood by everyone.

The Adjutant General, Jones, of General A. S. Johnston's staff, said to the generals, "You have your orders verbally. I have no time to make out written orders but will see that all have them by nightfall." (This report I have here before me with Colonel Jones's own signature.)

Now, let us see what happens. On the third day of April at high noon the Confederate army began moving out of Corinth. Commander General A. S. Johnston and Commander General Beauregard with their respective staffs did not start out until very late in the afternoon, supposing, of course, that the army was on the move and would be, by that time, almost to Monterey. What a surprise, after going a short distance in the wake of the army, to find everything standing still! They inquired and were told that those behind were waiting for the advance to move.

Beauregard sent an aide-de-camp to General Polk, riding up to the General, asking, "General, why are you not marching?" The General replied simply, "I am waiting for written orders." The day was closing, nightfall setting in, and the army went into camp not having yet reached Monterey. That was the beginning of a delay which seemed, to me, Providential.

Then what happened? Buell's army was on its way to Grant. The Confederates knew it and knew, also, that in order to attack Grant singly they would have to commence battle Friday morning.

Thursday brought the entire Confederate army to Monterey, still eleven miles from Pittsburg Landing. Friday morning the army started from Monterey. A portion of it had an engagement with some of General Sherman's Union troops. I remember, well, hearing the roar of cannon.

Simultaneously with this engagement, the heavens grew black with an oncoming storm which broke with another kind of thunder. Down came the rain, drenching the marching host of the Confederate army, impeding their progress, and making the roads almost impassable for artillery and heavy trucking such as the ammunition and supply trains. Night closed in, and they were not yet near the Union army.

Though Saturday opened up bright and fair, it took them until late afternoon to arrive where they could draw up their line, ready to give battle to the Union forces. They resolved not to attack until early daylight. 42,000 men would, then, move upon the unprepared enemy, who would be sleeping quietly in their tents. General Johnston felt confident of success. He was determined to see it through in order to retrieve the reverses of that Spring's campaign involving the loss of so many of his department, and also that he might remove the cloud cast on his name by the criticism from the Southern people.

That evening, there was a conference of the leading Confederate generals. General Beauregard made the suggestion that inasmuch as they had lost two days so that the Union Army must be apprised of their presence and be ready for them, and since in all probability General Buell must have already arrived, it would be better for the Confederates to turn back to Corinth, fortify themselves more securely, and fight the Union army on the defensive.

General Johnston said that, while he considered all that General Beauregard had said, yet the army was now in the presence of their enemies, and he was resolved to give battle. He declared he would fight them if they were a million. The Union army, he was sure, could not present a stronger front than he could. And with this decision, the Confederate generals settled down to wait until the first streak of light to pounce on their unsuspecting enemy.

Pre-Dawn Patrol

The Union army were sleeping in their tents, and yet in a portion of that army there was some stir, for the Lieutenant Colonel of our regiment could not rest. He felt oppressed by some unseen impending danger and resolved to impress our division commander with the defenseless condition of our army. The upshot of it was that a force of two-hundred men, a portion of the 25th Missouri. Infantry and also the same from the 12th Michigan Infantry, were told to reconnoiter our front. I am now speaking from my own experience. I was one of that number. We were roused a little after midnight to fall in line. The captain counted us off. He allowed those to fall out who did not feel well. I would have been excused as I was cook that week for the squad I belonged to, but I decided to go. After waiting some time at headquarters, we, at last, started out, about two-hundred strong.

The stars were shining, and, as nearly as I could judge, it must have been about three o'clock in the morning. We reached our picket line which was only a short distance. Here we were divided into three squads. Major Powell of the 25th Missouri Infantry was commanding, by order of Colonel Peabody. I have a typewritten account of how Colonel Peabody, on his own responsibility, ordered out his force, saying to one of his officers, before the move was made, that he would not live to see the result of it. He was right. Not more that four hours from that time, he was shot from his horse, dead.

But to return to our scouting expedition, we started off in our three squads through the woods in, what seemed to me, as nearly as I could judge, a southwesterly direction. Once or twice, we came to an opening and saw log cabins which were deserted, though we heard the crowing of fowl. At one time in the darkness, we came near opening fire on our own men of the party to our right who were coming toward us. Had one of our: rifles been discharged, there would have been a slaughter, and the enemy would have been apprised of our coming. Again we separated, when presently we came upon an open spot in the timber. When we halted, the first streak of daylight had appeared, and we noticed at a short distance a rise of ground which seemed to be covered with thick underbrush.

As we watched, we noticed something white moving through the brush, and in another moment, we spied a horseman whose movements we made out to be those of an enemy. Our captain, at once, ordered our counter march to the rear, but we had no sooner got well started than the crack of several muskets was heard, and bullets were soon whizzing after us. I still feel queer when I think what the result would have been, had we walked, unawares, straight into the battle lines of 42,000 of the enemy!

Knowing Nothing

We soon were forming with the other squads in skirmish lines, advancing, firing, then taking cover wherever we could. The enemy was yet out of sight, hidden in the timber and brush, and we could only direct our fire toward the flash from their guns. Several of our force were already wounded, one mortally. However, we kept moving forward. As Dr. Kedzie has said, "Knowing nothing, we feared nothing." We had now covered quite a space in advancing, and as the rattling of musketry became thicker and faster, it became evident that there must be quite a force in front of us. As I took cover behind a tree, hardly large enough to cover me, and kept busily firing, several enemy bullets were driven into the tree about at the line of my head. One just clipped by my right ear. Evidently someone took me for a good mark.

Daylight, Day One

Daylight now came streaming through the woods. There was a short lull in the firing, and looking off to the left front, I discovered a cavalry force moving to our left. I called the attention of Major Powell to them and suggested that perhaps they were endeavoring to flank us. He watched them a moment and decided that was what they were trying to do, whereupon he called his bugler and immediately sounded the retreat. As soon as that movement began, the enemy followed, pouring a galling fire upon us. We were endeavoring to carry off our wounded, and so our progress was slow. We had not retreated far when we met Colonel Moore of the 21st Missouri.

Infantry with five companies of his regiment. He rated us as cowards for retreating. We warned him not to be too bold, or he would get into trouble. It was not twenty-five minutes after that when he was wounded twice and his force nearly annihilated or put to rout. Major Powell endeavored to hold back the enemy but could not stand against them. Our battle lines gave way, and the Major himself was killed before we reached camp.

As soon as the enemy got within sight of our camp, they began to come on with renewed strength. Doubtless, the commanders were satisfied that we were unprepared to meet them. I have mentioned that I was cook for my squad during the week of the battle. After I reached camp, carrying a wounded man, I picked up a pail and started for water at the Rhea Springs, not supposing, even then, that the enemy would drive us from our camp. About half a mile on my way to the spring, I stepped out to a clear field where there was a camp of the 53rd Ohio Infantry. A group of soldiers had gathered looking westward across a ravine from which continued fighting could be heard. In another instant, the quartermasters came riding in from the south and reported that the Confederate army were coming in force, that Colonel Moore's men were routed and in retreat, and that Colonel Moore had been wounded twice.

I looked across the ravine, saw the battleline of the Confederates, and started on a run toward the spring for my pail of water. Arriving there, I found men, in crowds, from Sherman's division at the Shiloh Church, getting water and watering horses and mules. I dipped my pail of water and started back towards our camp. I had gone but a short distance when, on looking back, I saw men, horses, and mules on a run—a perfect rout. The Confederate line had already appeared, and yet none of Sherman's men were in line. As I came in sight of the camp of the 53rd, up in the field, that regiment was forming in line of battle on the edge of the timber just east of their camp. I had not gone far before this regiment began firing, and the bullets whistled by me. I held on to my pail of water until I arrived at our tent.

Our division was out in line of battle a little distance in advance on a rise of ground. The Confederate lines were pouring a withering fire into our Army. Already, men were leaving the lines. Many wounded were drifting through camp to the rear. I went into the tent, set down my pail, filled my canteen, and got my gun and accoutrements, for it did not look as though there would be any breakfast. Bullets were riddling the tent, and as I stepped out, I saw our men wavering. The battle line was breaking. Both of Prentiss's lines gave way and broke for the rear, as well as Sherman's division. Some distance to our rear, we reformed. Just as the new lines began to form, the artillery began work. I halted where the new lines were, but many pushed on through to the rear, and I did not see them come into the battleline that day.

The battle soon became general, and I need not speak any further on the progress of this terrible conflict which lasted all that Sunday, April 6, 1862. Enough has been written so that anyone interested may easily be informed of all that went on. The day closed with the Union army still holding sufficient ground to stand. I stayed in the line until I lost every comrade of my company. I took part in the last effort we made to repel the Confederate army. Exhausted at length, I lay down on the bare ground that Sunday night, under one of the large siege guns up on the bluff above the river, and went to sleep. This cannon was covered with a canvas. I looked out and saw the stars shining. The battle had closed for that night, and only an occasional shell from the gunboats came crashing through the timber.

Sometime during the night, I woke up and turned over. Something cold was on my shoulders. It felt like water. Feeling around, I discovered that it was a little rivulet, and that it was running under my body down the bluff into a deep ravine. I sat up, resting my head on my knees, and looked out from under the canvas. It was raining. What a godsend to both Blue and Gray, lying wounded out on the battlefields! It stopped the fire which the shells had started at many points in the dry grass and also provided water for the parched throats of those who could move only a few inches

Bloody Day Two

With the light of another day, the battle again resumed, and with three fresh divisions of Buell's army which had joined us, and with Lew Wallace's division and the broken organization of Grant's army, the contest was resumed in full fury. Crawling out from under my shelter, I moved down to where I could fill my canteen with dirty Tennessee water and a few hardtacks. I fell in with a portion of our regiment that our Lieutenant Colonel Graves had picked up, and we marched out again to the battleline. We were attached to a portion of Buell's men, as a reserve.

Confederates Retreat

By two o'clock, with occasional downpours of rain, the Confederates gave up the struggle and began their retreat back to Corinth. They showed themselves a wiser but sadder army and left us master of the field of human slaughter. We followed up the retreating army and found, among the fallen, Blue and Gray intermingled. Some were cold and stark in the embrace of death; some were breathing out their lives. Thousands of them had lain there all night, torn and bleeding, with no hand to lend assistance.

One day not long ago when the Armistice of the World War was being celebrated, I heard two ladies talking. One of them was saying: what a terrible war this last one had been. The other answered that the Civil War was a terrible war, too. "Yes," said the first woman, "but that was only a picnic." If that lady had walked with me on that Monday afternoon close upon the retreating Confederates, she would never have wanted to witness another such "picnic."

There is one experience I would like to speak of in particular: I came upon three Confederate soldiers, two of them wounded so sorely that they were just breathing their last. One was a beardless boy, not more than fourteen or fifteen years old. He was sitting, leaning up against a tree, and as I approached him he called out in a clear voice:

"Well, if you are going to kill me, kill me."

I asked, "Why do you think I want to kill you?"

He answered, "Our folks say that you kill all the prisoners."

I replied, "Yes, your people have told you many things. They would make us out savages."

"But what are you going to do with me?" he asked.

"Why," said I, "the ambulances are out picking up all the wounded, and they will come for you, too."

A piece of shell had shattered his hip, and he could not rise upon his feet. Just then an ambulance came near, and I called their attention to this severely wounded boy.

He continued saying, like all the people did down there, "What you'se come down to fight we-uns for? If you want the niggers I wisht you had all of them. I haven't got any."

When he asked again what would be done with him, I told him that when they came after him, he would, no doubt, be taken aboard the hospital boat lying in the Tennessee River where he would receive attention. He said he had a mother in Illinois and wanted to know if he would be allowed to see her. I told him I thought so, and that if ever he reached her, I'd advise him to stay there. Again assuring him that he would certainly be cared for when the ambulance returned, I left him. I have wondered, many a time, whether he ever reached his mother.

My fellow comrades had now left me, so I plodded my way towards our camp which the Confederates had captured and occupied the day before. Here and everywhere, the battle strife was evident. Of course, our camps were rifled of everything that could be carried away. Some of our tents were burned, mine among them. Just on the right of our camp, I saw the dead body of Colonel Peabody, Commander of our brigade. He had evidently been shot from his horse, for he lay with his legs across a log and his head and shoulders on the ground. All the buttons and shoulder straps had been cut from his clothes.

It was growing dark, and but few of the regiment had arrived at the camp. Most of them started back to the river. Here I had another melancholy experience, for as I tramped over the battlefield, thick with darkness and occasional rain, I stumbled over something, and bending down to see more distinctly, I found myself looking into the face of a dead soldier. I hurried on, reached the Landing, and there I found what was certainly a conglomerate host—soldiers from every army of the service hunting and inquiring for their comrades! I found two or three of mine, and we proceeded to find a place to lie down and get some needed rest. We found some straw and spread it under a baggage wagon that would keep us up out of the mud. There we lay down and slept, while the rain kept steadily on.

Burying the Dead

Next morning, we crawled out from under our partial shelter, filled our canteens with Tennessee water, muddy from the rains, and with a few hardtacks, settled down to our "picnic" breakfast.

These were the common experiences which every soldier in the war had to meet. After breakfast, we went again to the battlefield and to our camp where we resumed our duties as a regiment organization. We buried our dead, cared for the wounded, and numbered our total loss at 192. Our division being badly torn by this battle, we were assigned to John A. Logan's division and encamped with them.

Misery

It seemed to us that all the clouds in the universe had gathered over Western Tennessee and were sending down a continual deluge which, at times, we felt was cold enough to freeze. We lacked the most necessary things—supplies, medical facilities, and hospitals. Things began to tell on our army. As we moved toward Corinth, we had to leave the sick behind at every step. The only thing to do with them was to send them north by steamboat, even though there was very inadequate medical attention given to them on board. Many died before they arrived.

Conditions in the army grew worse every day. We were constantly moving, perhaps only a few miles at a time, and our supply and baggage trains were often mired so that they could not come up with us for days. Meanwhile, we would be left without shelter, food, or hospital care, and this soon caused nearly all to become sick. Stomach trouble, diarrhea, fever, and chills soon brought a large share of our army to the point where they were in no shape for offensive service against any enemy.

General H. W. Halleck now arrived from headquarters at St. Louis, Missouri and took command in person, but I doubt whether any of the rank and file believed that conditions were bettered thereby. His commanders and army generally believe, to this day, that he could have captured Beauregard's army and not have allowed them to get away.

What is Left of the 12th?

No soldier who served in that campaign will ever forget it. Our own regiment, the 12th Michigan Infantry, got so reduced by sickness and death on account of exposure and hardship that General Logan sent us back to the river to recruit. But alas! That was no place to recruit. Sick soldiers as we were, scores died, and many were sent home. There was no building for a hospital, nor physicians to care for us, nor needed medical supplies. I myself was sick for three weeks and became so weak that I despaired of my life and felt I would never see home again.

He is Watching

But He who cares for all His children must surely have been watching over me, for I recovered slowly. Many years later, I-offered up my thanks to Him as I knelt on that battlefield on the 54th anniversary of that terrible conflict.

Chapter Four

Marching

About the first of June, the weather began to grow hot. We were glad to be ordered to march away from the place. The heat had killed some of the horses, and even the bodies of some of the soldiers, in their shallow rain-washed graves, sent a strong odor over the battlefield.

Although yet very weak to march, we were glad to get away out into purer air and where people lived. A two days' march brought us to Bethel on the Mobile and Ohio Railroad, north of Corinth, Mississippi, about twenty-two miles. Footsore and so tired I threw myself down on the ground without trying to get anything to eat. We rested here for a few days. There was a beautiful spring where we got water that seemed exceedingly refreshing. And the vegetables were so much more palatable than hardtack, pork, and coffee.

After about a week, we moved on north to Jackson, Tennessee. The heat was severe, and we were tired and footsore so we turned into a grove to lie down on the bare ground. A sudden wind from the northeast came up, and the weather turned chilly. The next day, we were on our way to another camp near the 43rd Illinois Infantry who were all Germans. Our duties were not very heavy—only guard and picket duty, so we began to be somewhat refreshed and strengthened.

Our regiment was very much reduced on account of the battle. Besides killed and wounded, nearly a hundred had been taken prisoners. Our tent quarters were no longer crowded. Whereas before, there were from twenty-two to twenty-four in a tent, there were now only twelve or fifteen. As we became stronger, we began to better our conditions by learning of camp and field service, taking advantage of all we had learned by sad experience. Officers and soldiers were becoming, every day, more used to the soldier's life and better acquainted with its duties.

Of course, it can be expected that among so many men of different character and training, there would be a few whose conduct brought down upon them some pretty severe punishments. Yet, in the main, we did not clear away everything in our way and tried, always, to have due regard for women and children who sometimes were left in destitute circumstances on account of the war.

July 1862

About the first of July that year of 1862, our Company D was detailed to go some thirty or forty miles north on the M. and O. Railroad not far from a place called Humboldt, Kentucky. We were sent out on flat cars and encamped near a cypress swamp. We were to guard the railroad which was in danger of being destroyed by the enemy. Our duty was mainly guard duty. We were out in the open country with patches of timber around us. Berries and vegetables were becoming ripe, and we occasionally had something quite palatable added to our coarse, army rations. Nothing unusual occurred during our stay of three or four weeks.

My most thrilling experience happened to me once, on picket duty. It was midnight, and I was standing under one of those large cypress trees whose branches spread out far and wide, almost hanging to the ground. Everything was as quiet as the grave when, all at once, the branches began to move about me. One of those large southern owls sent forth his most unearthly whoop. It made the woods resound far and wide and fairly lifted the hair from my head. At least, a large share of my hair came out that summer. While the cause was probably a touch of typhoid fever, still the owl's hoot may have helped.

Bolivar

When we were relieved, we boarded a train of flat cars to return to our regiment. During our stay at Humboldt, the regiment had moved further south from Jackson to a place called Bolivar, some forty-five miles distant. We arrived there about 8:30 in the evening and unloaded our baggage at the railroad depot.

The Lieutenant in charge asked us if we desired to march out to the camp or whether we would rather stay at the depot. We told him we would rather stay there until morning as it was a mile and a half out.

Presently our acting orderly, Thompson, detailed me and Comrade Long for guard over the baggage. We two stayed up with each other nearly all night. In the morning, after taking a lunch for breakfast, we marched over to the camp on Bright's Hill in the open. It was now late in July or near the first of August, 1862. It began to be fiercely hot. We had not been more than half an hour in camp before the regular Orderly Sergeant came around making up a detail for fatigue duty. He told me I was one of those detailed to go.

Severe Test

Here came one of the severest tests in my military life. My rights as a private soldier were at stake. I had just been discharged from my duty as a guard during the night and needed my rest. I knew it was contrary to army regulations to force a man on duty until his regular turn came, unless for violation of some military rule in which case, as a punishment, a private could be placed on extra duty. I knew I did not belong in that class, and to surrender to an arbitrary command did not fit me very well. After I informed the sergeant and proved that I had just come from guard duty, he not only persisted in his orders but swore at me. That overbalanced my good nature. I saw there was no use discussing things further with him, so I asked him to go to and see what he had to say. The sergeant claimed that he had left off at my name when our company was sent away on detached service. I knew there was no argument in that and stood my ground. I told my story to the captain who sidestepped by saying he did not wish to interfere with the orderly sergeant's department.

I knew he was only evading his duty as captain in performing a just act for one of the soldiers of his company. We were at a standstill. There was one higher court of appeal, and for a moment, I was inclined to take it. Had I appealed to the colonel of our regiment, I am almost sure I should have had a hearing. But this would have placed the orderly and the captain in a humiliating position, especially as considerable antagonism existed at the time between the colonel and the captain.

My better judgment told me that, if I went to the colonel, it would be taken as an act of revenge. I was a private, and I knew it would put me under the displeasure and surveillance of my superiors. So I resolved to bide my time and told them I would go if this was their sense of justice. I joined the squad, taking along my spade to help dig the sinks.

The sergeant in charge of this Detail was quite a different man. After arriving at the place where we were to work, the sergeant divided his squad into two reliefs, one and two, changing every half hour. As I came in number two, I sat down by the side of the sergeant and related my experience of the morning.

He said to me, "And they sent you out here to work in the hot sun after coming from guard duty?"

I said, "Yes, and I can prove it, if you wish to take the trouble to go with me."

"No," he answered, "you are all right. Take your spade and go back to your company. If they say anything to you, tell them I sent you. I'm in command today."

I obeyed the sergeant, picked up my spade, and returned to my company. It was no more than fifteen minutes before the orderly sergeant came around and wanted to know if I had reported with my Detail. I told him I had, and he asked, "Then why aren't you with them?"

"Because," I said simply, "the sergeant sent me back. He said you had no right to put me on duty when I came off from guard, and he is in command today."

This was too much for the orderly sergeant and he walked off. I have been particular in relating this experience because I am fully satisfied that it favored my military prospects afterwards, when that very same Sergeant recommended me for promotion and the captain afterwards for a Commission.

Foraging

Our duties here were principally guard and picket duty, some reconnoitering, and now and then a foraging expedition. One of these I will relate. A detail of soldiers was made the evening previous to our going. We were to be ready early in the morning, and accordingly reported at headquarters to receive orders. We had to wait quite a while, and so some of the boys went on a personal foraging expedition of their own. A case of wine bottles which, no doubt, belonged to some of the headquarters officers, had been left carelessly sticking out from under the tent. The boys pulled it out but had no corkscrew to open the bottles. As a substitute, they took the draw pin from the wagon tongue and thus knocked the heads of the bottles off and imbibed from the necks of the bottles. Of course, the teamsters who were always in the lead in anything of this kind got their fair portion. While no irregularities occurred, we all got enough for the work on hand.

Yankee Linkum Soldier

We passed on out into the country some five or six miles and turned into a large plantation where we loaded the wagons with oat bundles and corn fodder. After that, we all went searching for personal forage. Jumping down from the wagons, some of the men went off after the poultry. I could hear the squawking and started in the direction of the racket, trotting along a path down in front of the slave cabin. An old gray-headed man was sitting in front of one of the cabins. He heard me coming but could not see me for he was nearly blind. Evidently, he had found out that "Yankee Linkum soldiers" were somewhere on the plantation and he intercepted me with, "Look-a-heah, you come heah!"

I stepped up to the old man and asked him what he wanted.

"Is you one of them 'Linkum soldiers'?"

I told him I was, and he asked me to step up closer. He could not see very well, he explained. So I came closer, and he took a good look up and down.

Suddenly, he exclaimed, "Well ah declah. You look like gentlemen. I believes you is gentlemen. Our folks said you had horns!"

I hastened to assure him that we were not of the horned tribe and were really quite civilized.

With that I started off, for the rest of the soldiers were getting all the chickens. I had to content myself with some peaches and watermelons, but they tasted mighty good. I have been particular in relating this incident because it is typical of many which occurred while we were camped on Bright's Hill at Bolivar. Most of us were farmer boys, and we knew what cows were for, especially that they needed milking every so often. When the blacks came after the cows, it was necessary for them to drive the animals past the picket post. The pickets saw to it that the cows were detailed long enough so that the day's milk supply was secured. Then, on the way to the barnyard, the herd had to pass our camp. Some of our spry milkers came in for their share. I'm inclined to think that by the time the cows reached Mr. Bright's barnyard there wasn't much milking left to be done. In addition to that, a man named Hunt would get up about three o'clock in the morning and relieve quite a number of the cows from their burdens. He used to sell the milk to the soldiers.

Another incident also concerns the cows: Mr. Bright owned a tannery, and one day one of our soldiers came upon a squad of Union cavalry who had killed a "critter" and were in the act of dressing it, out in the pasture. They were just taking off the hide when this soldier inquired if he could have it. The others were interested in the meat and parted easily with the hide. The soldier took it, rolled it into a pack, and brought it to Mr. Bright's tannery. Mr. Bright being present, the soldier offered the hide for sale. Mr. Bright examined it carefully and said it looked like a hide from off his own cattle. This resulted in some parleying, but in the end the soldier disposed of the hide to Mr. Bright for $2.50. I am not sitting in judgment on the soldier's act. To many such as he, it was "war" and no time to question right or wrong.

We were sometimes sent out as a reconnoitering party and sometimes called into the line of battle expecting to fight. Later, we again moved to another camp some distance north of Bolivar.

Company D was here for a time, detached again, and posted in a fort in which was stationed a battery of artillery.

Dangerous Train Rides and Weary Marches

About the middle of September, our regiment was sent to Corinth, Mississippi as reinforcement to General Rosecrans at the Battle of Iuka, Mississippi. We broke camp early in the morning and proceeded to where we could wait for a train north to Jackson, Tennessee and then to Corinth. We waited all day, and the train did not come until morning.

We arrived at Corinth about dark, and here we were reminded of the condition of southern railroads, riding inside and on top of box cars. At Corinth, we were switched over on the Memphis and Charleston Railroad. The train consisted of about fifteen cars. Out of Corinth, we encountered a grade which the engine endeavored to make three different times, all ineffectually. At last, they resorted to cutting off a few cars and started on. Thus, portions of this train were left along the track. When at last the engine went on, I was on top of a box car of one section. I stretched out and got to sleep, having been tossed about all day on top of the car.

I could not have slept more that a half hour when a dash of rain came pouring down on us. We crowded down below to get inside when already it was filled like a box of sardines. No rest nor sleep for any of us. It continued to rain all night and next forenoon.

Sometime before noon, the railroad engine returned from Burnsville, picked up the sections left on the track, and pushed back into Corinth. Here we succeeded in getting a war dinner; and sometime after, the train was made up again. We boarded it, and the engine put on all steam to make the grade. I was sitting in the car door and looking off across the fields when, all at once, my feet struck the end of a stick of timber. As good fortune would have it, my feet flew up and slid along on top of this timber fairly making the sparks fly. Simultaneously, with the jerk it gave my feet, a strong hand was laid on my shoulder, and the strength of it lifted me up bodily onto my feet.

The Lieutenant stood there in front of me and said with a nervous tremor, "You d_ _ , you came near getting killed." I didn't disagree with him, for I am sure that if my feet had been drawn under the timber instead of over, I should never have been able to tell the story.

We moved out to the battlefield and remained in line of battle, but not called into action. Next morning we moved back to Burnsville and marched back to Corinth. This was a tedious march for the weather was hot. We arrived at Corinth and returned by train to Bolivar by way of Jackson.

Next day, as we were pulling out of Jackson, we were in for real trouble. At the rear of the train were three flat cars and one passenger coach. Two of the cars were not crated in. The one that Company D was on was crated. The soldiers, mostly the 68th Ohio Infantry, were sitting on the car hanging their feet off. The train was under good headway, and as we passed a switch, all at once these flat cars jumped the track, swaying to and fro. The soldiers commenced to jump. A number did not clear the car and were run over and killed. This accident seemed worse than a battle and cost, at least, four or five lives. The railroads in the South, at the time of the war, were in terrible condition.

We arrived back at Bolivar that evening having traveled, by marches and railroad, about 175 miles. We were glad enough to get back to camp for here it was mainly camp and picket duty.

Chapter Five

Battle of Corinth

About this time, the campaign against Vicksburg was commenced under General Grant. New regiments were constantly being sent south over the railroad to Holly Springs, Mississippi. The Battle of Corinth was on under General Rosecrans, the first of October. An order came to Bolivar for a Division to intercept the Confederate army retreating from Corinth after the battle. We started on the morning of the second. I had just been put on picket duty the night before, and after traveling about until nearly midnight and posted from 12:00 to 2:00 o'clock was again recalled and relieved by another force and ordered to return to camp. Arriving in camp, I found the regiment preparing to march. I had scarcely time to eat, put some rations into my haversack, and fall into line for the march.

One of the most trying experiences of a soldier is when he is hurried into line for the march and has to either stand with all his accouterments on the wait or else loiter along the road until the sun is pretty well up, and then get into double quick with the members of the General's staff galloping around on horses and urging speed.

We marched on all that day and the next, and about evening we filed into a swamp and were apprised that we were very near the enemy. We were allowed no lights or fire and were to make absolutely no noise.

Early next morning we were aroused and, from all actions, soon surmised there was something to be done. As we filed into the road, we heard cannonading and before long came up with the enemy. The larger part of the enemy was on the east side of the Hatchee River while small portions had come over onto the west side. We were filed into a cotton field and there formed in line of battle. One of our batteries was planted on a rise of ground to our front and left and had a lively engagement with one of the Confederate artilleries.

We were put in motion down the cotton field and over quite a rise of ground through a grove of timber. We crossed a road over a fence into a cornfield.

By this time, some of the Confederate artillery were directing their fire upon us. We made a lively hustle over the fence and while I was getting over it a cannonball struck the panel of fence from under me. I did not stand on the order of my going but made at once for lower ground where their balls flew over our heads. One of our batteries, being planted on the rise of ground we had just passed over, commenced work upon the Confederate batteries.

That put us under crossfire, but, fortunately, it all went over our heads as we were now all pretty well on the flat of the river bottom. After scaling fences, jumping ditches, and tearing my clothes, I came upon a grove of oaks. We had hardly entered the grove when our Colonel yelled for us to drop. Scarcely had we struck the ground before a shower of bullets went over us. Those who were responsible for the volley were hidden in the lane, but when they saw us up and after them, they climbed the fences and got away in short order. On we went, but they got out of sight, and we paused on the riverbank wondering what was to come next. Presently our Colonel W. H. Graves who had now become our full Colonel since Colonel Quinn resigned said to us, "Boys, there is a brigade down north of here about half a mile. Several regiments are standing there hesitating to cross. Knowing full well that the Confederates have already covered that bridge and are awaiting the first troops to blow them into atoms, I have asked the General for the privilege of leading my regiment across. Will you follow me if I go ahead?" he asked.

We all called out with one accord, "Go ahead. We'll follow you."

The order was given to left face, double quick, and shout. We started down along the riverbank. The troops nearest the bridge, hearing us and not wanting to be outdone, started across ahead of us. Immediately, the Confederate batteries let loose upon them with grape and canister. When they got across the bridge, they swung to the right. At this point, there was a short bend in the river and, there, those troops were unmercifully cut to pieces. As we swung down onto the bridge, grape and canister were racking it.

I remember seeing by the bridge an oak tree, partly hollow, into which a little black boy had crowded himself, all shivering with fright. There he crouched in terror while the bullets tore the bark from the tree and made the slivers fly.

General Hurlbut, on horseback, was urging us to cross the bridge, and you can imagine there was no loitering! As we reached the other side, we swung to the left where the banks were somewhat steep. I reached to take hold of a soft maple sapling to swing myself up. A grape shot struck the top of it, just above my head, cut it off and sent it flying over into the river. Had the bullet struck a little lower, or my head been a little higher, I would not have gone clambering on up the embankment with my comrades.

We came out into a field, and fortunately, the enemy's fire had begun to slack up. Evidently they saw we were likely to outflank them, and so they left their guns which fell into our hands. A small force of the enemy was still disputing our advance, but our own batteries, coming up, soon silenced theirs. This closed the battle.

We had captured thirteen cannons in all and some five-hundred prisoners. The Confederate army made its escape by crossing the river at a ford. We knew that we had gained a signal victory for the Union and defeated the Confederate forces in their plans.

None were killed in our regiment, but a few were wounded, and a piece of shell had torn our flag. The color bearer was among those wounded. Our regiment was fortunate, for the Union forces, as a whole, sustained some heavy losses.

Our regiment was appointed to guard the prisoners back to Bolivar, and we did it in good shape on two days' march. Then we felt like settling down for a good rest, as our recent encounter had been a "hurry-up" of five or six days. We now occupied our former camp with the usual camp duties.

Meanwhile troops were still being pushed south, concentrating for the Vicksburg campaign.

Now and then, while in camp, our regiment sent out a foraging expedition to secure forage for the teams. Whole trains of wagons would drive into a cornfield and load up forage. Of course, we would get our share whenever there was anything left! Usually, the cavalry got in ahead of us.

Chapter Six

November 1862

Late in November of the year 1862, another march was ordered for our division, the 61st Illinois and the 12th Michigan Infantry, acting as rear guard. We started early in the morning of a fine day warm for that season of the year.

It frequently happened on such an occasion that the whole column of march got strung out twice as long as it should be. Then about ten or eleven o'clock, the staff officers would come galloping down the line to close up the ranks. Since we came behind all the artillery, baggage, and ambulances, it usually meant that by the time the closing up reached the rear we were put into double-quick time. But this day, Colonel Fry of the 61st Illinois Infantry was in command, and he did not propose to start his men on the run in the heat of the day. He kept us on our usual route step. When it came noon and we found a good place to halt for dinner, we halted though the other portion of the army had gotten quite a distance in advance.

At night we halted in a field of cotton near LaGrande, Tennessee. We had made a forced day's march of twenty-two miles and were tired enough to lie down anywhere. There were some five-hundred acres of cotton, and the fields were as white as driven snow. Of course, a large portion of this was destroyed by the tramp of horses, men, and wagons.

Our entire expedition seemed more like a reconnoiter than anything else. Our movements were directed against the enemy's cavalry, and so our infantry forces were practically useless. There was nothing to do but turn around and march back to Bolivar. To retrace those twenty-two miles, without seeming to have accomplished anything, was not inspiring.

Marching Through Wet Sticky Clay

Next morning about 9 o'clock, after considerable dilatory waiting, we were put on the return march.

The sky began to grow dark and lowering, betokening the coming of a storm, and about eleven o'clock, the storm broke. It did not come with a rush but steadily increased in volume as the minutes passed. We were marching through red Tennessee clay which shortly began to be sticky and very adhesive. At times, our shoes would load so badly, we fairly stuck fast. By reason of this, we were forced to take them off, tie them together, and carry them strung upon our guns. As the rain continued, our clothing was drenched until I felt the moisture drizzling along my spine. Still, we kept plodding along. We would not stop to eat, and whatever we carried in our haversacks was soaked to mush by this time.

About five o'clock, some six or seven miles from Bolivar, we passed apiece of timber and came upon General Ross and his staff. They had built up a great fire of fence rails around which they stood trying to dry themselves. Their clothes were smoking from the heat. This looked quite inviting, and General Ross asked us if we wished to stay there or move on to camp at Bolivar. We told him we had decided to go on into camp, and so we kept plodding along with wet clothes, aching limbs, and sore feet. The wet ground did not look very inviting to sleep on. A cold wind had come up from the northwest, and we had to keep on the move. The general told us to go the best way we could, and so, presently, when we came out onto the railroad, some turned off and followed it while others kept on along the highway.

As we neared Bolivar, we got scattered and separated. My feet were very sore, and I fell somewhat to the rear. It had grown dark, and we were uncertain of surrounding objects. I traveled along the railroad track and came upon a trestle way. It was some distance across, and after going only a little way, I turned back for fear that in the darkness I should make a misstep, be hurled below, and get injured or killed. I turned to go down the bank which was quite steep. I had hardly gotten started before my feet slipped, and I rolled like a barrel down the bank, some fifty or sixty feet. As I went, I gathered to myself more and more of the Tennessee clay until I reached the bottom. When I endeavored to get up, I could hardly rise. I lay there for some time trying to remove some of the burden. When at last I got upon my feet, I shook myself as a horse would, then plodded on toward camp.

Arriving there, wet, hungry, tired, and shivering with cold, I lay down in my tent. Daylight came, and we looked out to find it snowing. It is needless to say that this exposure to the weather was a severe test upon our bodies and had its sad effects causing sickness and death. To some, it brought results from which they, then, suffered all their lives. We lost one of our company from this experience, William. Pincomb. He contracted diphtheria, and we laid him to rest in the local cemetery at Bolivar. His remains were removed later to the National Cemetery at Corinth, Mississippi.

I was able to visit his resting place in 1919. As I beheld the care with which the grounds and surroundings of that cemetery are tended, I said to myself, "Surely no nation has ever remembered her defenders as has the United States." The cemetery at Corinth is only one of the eighty-one national cemeteries where no expense has been considered too great in caring for these sacred grounds.

To my mind, the recent move, which had caused so much exposure and suffering with no compensating gain of any kind, lacked good military sense. Of course we were only in the first grip of the war and everything was in its experimental stage, lacking real military genius and management.

Chapter Seven

Guarding the Railroad

It was now getting near the close of the month of November. Cold nights and bad weather were setting in, and we moved again with the entire regiment along the Mississippi Central Railroad to a point about four miles south of Middleburg, Tennessee. We stayed there to guard the railroad near a deep gulch. From here companies were detached and posted along this railroad. Holding this road from the enemy was of great importance to General Grant's army in transporting troops and supplies.

Our Company D and Company H were sent back towards Bolivar, three companies stationed at Middleburg, three companies at the gulch, and two companies at Hickory Valley. Headquarters were established at Middleburg, and from there all reports and orders were received and sent out. Our two companies took quarters in a two-story frame building which was not occupied. Here we expected to rest and prepare for the winter. The ground was beginning to freeze, and there were occasional snow flurries. The building with its usual chimney and fireplace was arranged with two rooms above and two below. Company D occupied the east end, Company H the west. We prepared everything for winter and settled down. This filled out the first year of our military life.

Our duties here were principally to prevent the enemy from tearing up the railroad tracks, which would prevent the transportation of troops and necessary supplies. Later the enemy was successful in disrupting this railroad.

Weird Injury

An incident here, I must relate: In each of the rooms we occupied as our quarters, there was a fireplace. Plenty of firewood was always near by with which to heat our quarters. A fourth of a mile down the road was an old shop in which were piled up a number of wagon hubs of very large size. Several of these, we brought to our quarters and used as stools. They had a hole about an inch in diameter bored through them and stood about eighteen inches high. One morning I was in the act of cleaning my gun, my wipers, and wrenches, lying on one of these stools. A fellow comrade was poking around the fire, but I took no particular notice. He had dropped a cartridge down the base of one of these hubs. I had just turned to pick up something and had my face directly over the hub into which this soldier had dropped the cartridge. A live coal had been drawn from the hearth, and as the cartridge exploded, I received the full explosion in my face. The force and shock threw me onto the floor, and my face and eyes were so burned that I was temporarily blinded.

Some remedies were suggested, but, when our cook rushed into the kitchen and came back with a handful of flour and threw it into my face, it could not have burned worse had he used live coals. The pain was something severe for a time. As there was no doctor, we used such means as experience suggested. The pain caused by the "flour" remedy was severe, but the fire seemed drawn out by it. Gradually, the pain grew less though for three days I could not see. Later, by using some other applications, gradually the burning and soreness began to disappear. For some time, the powder remained in my eyeballs and on my forehead. The proceeding on the part of this soldier was unintentional, yet, at the same time, it needed its punishment from the viewpoint of carelessness. He was placed to perform my duties until I was well.

Playing a Trick

Another incident occurred to prove that a soldier's life is not made up entirely of dangers and dullness. Among so many different characters, there were always some that would bring out something to help cheer the monotony and dullness of camp life. Among our comrades, was one who had already reached bachelor years, and who yet had not altogether given up making himself quite agreeable to the ladies. He could not write his own letters, so he got others to do some correspondence to his girls. A comrade who lived in his vicinity at home had informed the others about the girl with whom he was corresponding. Of course, they put their wits together to play a trick.

It was three miles from our camp to Middleburg, Tennessee, where the headquarters of the regiment was established, from and to which we received and sent our mail. Every day a mail carrier was sent to take and receive mail for our two companies. The jokesters proposition was to write a letter as from the lady correspondent and place it in a former envelope with the address written by her to Milton H. Stout.

A few days before, some of the men had been out and killed a sandy pig, had brought it into camp, and dressed it. The young lady in question had red hair. To go out and select enough of this pig's bristles was but the work of a minute, and to weave it into a coil and place it in the letter was soon accomplished. An understanding was arranged with the mail man that he should place this letter in his pocket and then mix it with the returning mail.

The mail usually arrived at dark, so when the orderly sergeant called the roll he would distribute the mail, calling each man's name. Of course, this was all known with the squad to which our comrade belonged. The orderly sergeant called out, "Milton H., a letter."

Of course Milton was on taps for his letter, and of course, we all knew what was coming. So we skipped inside, and some of us climbed into our bunks. For fear I might let loose and not be able to contain myself, I stuck a comer of the blanket into my mouth. Comrade H. Henry Winfield, who had been doing Milton's corresponding, was sitting by our writing table. As Milton came in, full of glee, bearing the letter in his hand, we were nearly convulsed. He stepped up to the table upon which stood a lamp. Now Milton was somewhat nearsighted and had to hold the letter up close to the light to discover who it was from. We, of course, were all watching every move. Milton said in a rather subdued voice when he discovered who it was from, "Yes, it's from her."

That pretty near set us off. He tore open the envelope and pulled the wonderful missive out. Of course, out came, also, the coil of sandy bristles.

"Why, look, Milton, she's sent you some of her hair," Henry remarked.

Milton eagerly picked it up and holding it close to his eyes remarked in subdued tones, to Henry, "I declare, it does look like her hair."

The volcano of merriment and laughter knew no bounds. Some us jumped out of our bunks, hollered, and whooped. Poor Milton, fairly stunned, stood and looked on. But when one of the comrades called for the letter to be read, he began to wake up to what it all meant. Stepping up to Henry Winfield he declared with venom that could not be misunderstood, "Henry Winfield, I will never forgive you as long as I live. You are the one that has done all this."

Of course, all of this only increased the merriment. The motion had been made and seconded that the letter be read, but here I must stop. The experience gave occasion for a long train of fun, and from later evidence, we should infer that Milton stuck to his word in regard to Henry.

Chapter Eight

Defending the Railroad

The year of 1862 was now drawing to a close. During the war, it became evident that, with a campaign launched against Vicksburg by General Grant's army, there came constant danger that the Confederates might get in the rear of Grant's troops and tear up the railroad and thus separate him from his supplies and troops. Towards the latter part of December, these operations began to be launched by Confederate General Forrest, near Jackson, Tennessee. He destroyed part of the railway, and another force started under General Van Dorn behind Grant's army. It succeeded in capturing Holly Springs, Mississippi, where a large quantity of supplies for the army was stored.

Either on account of inefficiency, or carelessness, and indifferent guard protection, this place was surrendered by Col. Murphy of the 8th Wisconsin Infantry which practically destroyed the possibilities of General Grant's attacking Vicksburg from the rear.

This same Confederate force kept marching northward and westward, and hints of their intention to strike at Bolivar were given us.

A portion of our regiment had been called to aid the force against General Forrest at Jackson, Tennessee. Our two companies were called in to Middleburg, while two or three companies still remained further south. Arriving at Middleburg, we immediately went to work to prepare for some defense by utilizing an old blockhouse, while others prepared a temporary fort at the railroad depot platform.

A force of General Hatch's cavalry arrived in Bolivar the night previous to that on which General Van Dorn got within three miles of Bolivar. But being apprised of the Union cavalry coming into Bolivar, Van Dorn changed his mind and turned southward along the railroad intending evidently to pick up everything that came his way.

The Fastest Horse

On the morning of his coming up the road to take in Middleburg, our Lieutenant Colonel was on his way to Bolivar to attend a court martial. He was on horseback and alone, and as he got about three miles out on the Bolivar road, he discovered a force on horses coming toward him over a hill. Feeling somewhat suspicious of their appearance even though they were wearing the blue overcoats of the Union army, he halted to investigate more closely. He decided they were Confederates and not Union soldiers. Wheeling his horse about, he started back towards Middleburg when a dozen or more of the advance of the enemy gave their horses the spur and started after him. The question was now a matter of who had the best horse. They sent volleys from their carbines.

A picket post just a mile east of Middleburg, composed of our men, got taken in. They were evidently too intent upon watching the race and forgot their own safety.

Colonel May had the best horse and came riding into town announcing to us that the Confederates were coming.

Surrender?

Colonel Graves and a number of us were playing ball when a rider was seen coming over the hill into town bearing a flag of truce. Colonel Graves met the horseman who, on his approach, demanded to know who was in command here.

Colonel Graves said, "I am," whereupon the rider announced his compliments from General. Van Dorn and demanded in a very impervious way that he surrender.

Colonel Graves replied that he had been stationed there to hold the place, not surrender it. The horseman turned, gave his horse the spur and the Confederates prepared for the attack.

Uneven Odds: 4000 to 115

There were between three and four thousand of the enemy, mostly mounted infantry. Every fourth man was detailed to hold the horses, and it was not long before a force on foot appeared over the hill to the east. They drew up in battleline by a rail fence and were in full view of the blockhouse in which Company D was stationed ready for them.

We had about thirty-five muskets. Col. Graves had placed himself on the platform of the railroad depot to give the signal to fire. At the north end of the depot was a large cotton platform. This had been made into a fort from which quite a body of men could fire. When everything was ready and the Confederate force was coming over the rail fence in line of battle, the Colonel gave the signal to fire from the blockhouse.

The force under the platform could not give their fire yet as the enemy was out of their range.

But following our first volley from the blockhouse, after the smoke had cleared away, it seemed as though the Confederates had all dropped into the ground. Of course, this volley from us was no doubt a great surprise for as they advanced boldly over the fence not a man of our force could have been seen.

Another Confederate force was brought up and turned down into the ravine. The force on the north side in full view of our guns had taken cover behind the houses indicated and in the gullies that ran down from the high ground. This afforded us only a chance shot when one showed himself from behind the building. But the force creeping along through the ravine came up against the bank of the railroad and there received another surprise. As they rose out of the ravine up onto the railroad, a tremendous volley from behind the railroad platform sent them back.

While we, from the blockhouse, could not see them in the ravine, except when they came upon high ground, we were always ready. A brick block, standing a little west from the railroad depot, had an outside stairway on the east side facing toward the Confederates. There was no opening on that side, only a door by which the upper story was reached.

The quartermaster of our regiment with several soldiers with guns and ammunition procured an iron bar, broke a hole through the wall large enough for a gun, and there several soldiers kept up a continual fusillade, as they had full view of the enemy.

During the firing, a Confederate soldier got down into a deep gully, stuck his hat on his bayonet up on the bank, and sat down about ten feet from it to watch the Yankees play bullets through it. I put several through it myself, and we began to make up our minds he was "coming roots" on us. We watched that spot carefully, and when the Confederates retreated we went out and found a Reb sitting there. He pointed to his hat and said we had spoiled it for him. We invited him to hand up his gun which he cheerfully did and surrendered himself as our prisoner, glad no doubt that his head had not been in the hat when we sent the bullets through it.

The Union cavalry had followed the Confederates out from Bolivar and were getting ready to charge them, so they took leg bail and left us master of the field. They reported the total loss as ninety men, killed, wounded, and prisoners. And they had not succeeded in tearing the railroad up.

This engagement with the enemy—so few of us (only 115 muskets in all) against so large a force of the Confederates—brought out a very complimentary order not only from our brigade commander but from General Grant who gave us praise for defending the post of Middleburg and thus keeping open the road by which supplies to the army were forwarded.

We remained at Middleburg a few days, then resumed our post of guarding the railroad between Bolivar and Middleburg. Since our old quarters had been burned by the enemy, we took up quarters at a little distance on a deserted plantation. There were buildings sufficient for quarters, and here we established our picket lines. And so we closed the first and, by far, the most severe year of our service. It had been a year of battles, severe marches, constant duties, privations, illness, and death. Yet through it all, I felt as though a Guiding Hand was leading the Union forces.

Editor's Notes

Dear Reader,

I presume that, like me, you wonder where you can read the rest of the story. I wondered what happened later. After an exhaustive search, I may have found the answer in a footnote. That is, the author, Joseph Ruff, must have died before finishing it. He wrote this story shortly before his death in 1921. Isn't it remarkable how sharp his memory remained?

Nevertheless, I learned a great deal about his life from his detailed obituary which is reprinted in this book. (See Obituary.)

Earlier, Joseph wrote another wonderful story about his life leading up to the war and how he came to America, entitled "The Joys and Sorrows of an Emigrant Family." [Ed: An excerpt from that book starts on page 58.]

Thank you to the Michigan Historical Society for kindly granting permission to republish my great-grandfather's remarkable story which originally appeared in the Michigan History Magazine. A footnote states that Joseph Ruff completed this manuscript shortly before his death, January 19, 1921.

If you know anything more about Joseph's Civil War experiences, or care to comment, feel free to email me at Dorothy@MercerPublications.com or sign my comment form on our website. www.MercerPublications.com.

Dorothy May Mercer, Editor and Publisher

Notes on the Author Joseph Ruff
Compiled by His Great Niece, Arlene O'Connell

Joseph Ruff was a commissioned officer when he was discharged after four years in the Union Army. After the Civil War, Joseph took a lively interest in Veterans' affairs and in 1890 became chairman of the Michigan Shiloh Soldiers' Monument Commission, a group dedicated to the erection of a monument on the 1862 battlefield in Tennessee.

The Commission failed in its first two efforts to get the Michigan Legislature to appropriate funds for the monument in 1894 and 1911, but the legislature of 1916-17 appropriated $4,500 for the monument. The monument, a granite structure topped by the figure of a soldier, was erected in October, 1918, and was dedicated by Joseph Ruff and other Michigan veterans on Memorial Day, May 30, 1919. The dedication program was opened by the singing of "The Star-Spangled Banner" by Ruff's daughter, Mrs. Viola Kingsnorth.

Ruff made this brief address, turning over the monument to the State of Michigan:

"Thank God that as we stand upon this sacred ground, made sacred by the sacrifice of so many of your noble sons of Michigan and other States, so long ago that the spirit of strife is past, we stand upon a firm foundation, a united nation.

"Doubly impressive, this Memorial Day, is the fact that garlands of flowers are placed upon the little green mounds of soldiers, dead of both North and South, as the nation's defenders not only in this nation's cause but for the cause of freedom and brotherhood in the world at large. May God hasten the day when the cause of freedom shall triumph among all mankind."

Obituary

Joseph Ruff

Joseph Ruff was born in Obendorf, Germany, March 18, 1841 and departed this life January 19, 1921, aged 79 years, 10 months, and 1 day.

He was the son of Xavier and Catherine Ruff and was the oldest of a family of six children. He immigrated in America with his parents in 1853 and located at Buffalo, New York. Two years later he came to Michigan and settled in Concord and has lived in the vicinity of Albion and Concord ever since.

On December 17, 1861, he enlisted in the Union army at Albion and served four years and two months. He was commissioned First Lieutenant November 18, 1865, and was mustered out at Camden, Ark., February 15, 1866. He was a member of the local G.A. R[1]. and was commander for four years.

He was married to Miss Catherine Bugbee of Clayton, Mich., on December 3, 1868, and to this union were born seven children, all of whom are living [editor: in Michigan]: Mrs. Walter [editor: Millie] Dodes of Concord, Mrs. Otis [editor: Viola] Kingsnorth of Albion, Lorenzo J. Ruff, Eckford, Mrs. A.E. Adams, Marshall, Alva G. Ruff, Lansing, Bert Ruff, Marshall and Dr. L.A. [editor: "Lou"] Ruff, Marshall.

In early manhood he was converted [editor: from Catholicism] and united with the Methodist Protestant church and retained this membership until death. He was an active Christian worker and has superintended two Sunday schools at one time. He had also been given a license to preach and conducted services at Concord, Rice Creek and Eckford.

In 1912 Mrs. Ruff passed away, and in 1915 Mr. Ruff was united in marriage to Mrs. Mary Simmons, who survives him. Mr. Ruff was a devoted husband and father. He loved his God, his house, and his country, and sacrificed much for all of them.

---

[1] The Grand Army of the Republic (GAR) was a fraternal organization composed of veterans of the Union Army (United States Army) Union Navy (U.S. Navy), Marines and the U.S. Revenue Cutter Service who served in the American Civil War.

Besides a host of friends, he leaves to mourn his loss, his devoted wife, his loving children, nine grandchildren and three great-grandchildren, also two brothers, Augustus and Jacob Ruff, of Albion, and three sisters, Mrs. Julia Fritz, of Jackson, Mrs. Martha DeVinney and Mrs. Frank Durkee, of Albion.

The funeral service was held on Friday, January 21. A brief service was held from the home, 106 South Huron Street, [Albion] at 12:30, conducted by the Rev. A.E. Cameron.

The main service was held from the First Presbyterian church at one o'clock. Rev. I.H. Riddick spoke of the deceased as a comrade, and of his service in the Civil War. He spoke feelingly of the geniality, goodness, and patriotism of the deceased. Rev. Frederick R. Vine, of the Baptist church read the 90th Psalm and opening prayer.

Rev. A.E. Cameron preached the funeral sermon. One of the texts selected for the sermon was from 2 Timothy 2:3: "Thou therefore endure hardness as a good soldier of Jesus Christ." He spoke of four of the outstanding characteristics in the life of the deceased, which were: He was an ambitious man, a home loving man, a patriotic citizen, and a Christian man.

In closing his discourse the pastor referred to a touching incident in the life of the deceased that occurred only a few days before he took to his bed for the last time. It was on one of Mr. Ruff's last trips downtown. Meeting the pastor on the concrete bridge which spans the race near the Presbyterian church, he said: "If this is my last illness I want to leave this testimony behind: There is a place out yonder in that house of many mansions to receive my spirit, and there are loved ones waiting over there to welcome me to my eternal home."

Mrs. William A. Krenerick sang, "One Sweetly Solemn Thought," and "Face to Face [with Christ, My Savior]," and Miss Ruth Biggs sang the favorite hymn of the deceased, "O Love that Will Not Let Me Go."

The following named members of the American Legion were the pallbearers: Edgar Walker, Herbert Behling, Mm. Clark, George Wilkinson, Joseph Gallagher, and Eugene Behling.

Members of the local G.A.R. had charge of the burial service at Riverside cemetery, which was concluded with the blowing of taps. The Presbyterian church was filled with relatives, friends, and neighbors of the deceased and with members of the G.A.R. and of the American Legion. The floral offerings were many and beautiful.

Joseph Ruff

By Frank Passic, Albion Historian.

Morning Star May 29, 2011 Pg, 6
Portions reprinted by permission

When the Civil War began, local resident Phineas Graves raised a company of men in the Albion area to fight in the Union Army. Graves served as a professor at Ira Mayhew's Commercial College here, and later in 1867 was one of the organizers of the Albion Public Schools. The group of men joined the 12th Michigan Infantry at Niles on March 5, 1862 and was designated as Company D. Graves was named Captain of the unit, and his men went right into battle the following month. The company gained the nickname "The Union Clinchers of Albion." Under his command, the scouts of Captain Graves fired the first Union skirmish shots in the historic Battle of Shiloh very early on Sunday, April 6, 1862.

One of our local soldiers under Grave's command was Joseph Ruff (1841-1921). A native of Germany, he came to America as a child in 1851. Ruff served as a sergeant, and later lieutenant in the 12th Michigan Infantry. Ruff volunteered to be part of the three squads which were sent out at 3 o'clock in the morning on that fateful day to scout out the enemy. Thus began the Battle of Shiloh, and Albion was well represented there.

Before he died in 1921, Ruff compiled his memoirs of that terrible battle. These memoirs, entitled "Skirmishing at Shiloh," were published in Michigan History Magazine years later in 1943. They were later reprinted in the 1999 book by the Michigan Historical Center entitled "Michigan and the Civil War, an Anthology," pages 35-38. This book is still readily available today. Joseph also wrote an article for Michigan History Magazine in 1920 about German immigrants.

Following the War, Ruff returned to Albion. He became active in the local E. W. Hollingsworth Post No.210 of the Grand Army of the Republic, and even served as its commander. At the time of his death his obituary stated … He was interred in Riverside Cemetery, just west of the cemetery office.

Sneak Peek

Dear Reader,

Thank you for reading this exciting book. We hope you enjoyed it. You may be interested in Joseph Ruff's previous account of his journey to America, with his family, in 1853. The true story of their harrowing crossing of the Atlantic, jammed like sardines into the hold of a sailing ship, may raise the hairs on the back of your neck. Here is a short excerpt from *The Joys and Sorrows of an Emigrant Family,* by Lt. Joseph Ruff.

Chapter 4 Sailing

At last, everything was ready to sail, and about one o'clock on the seventh day, our vessel was towed out of the harbor through a stream into the English Channel. As soon as there was sea room enough for sailing, the sailors spread their canvas, the tugs released their charge and returned to port, leaving us to roam the ocean free.

The John Ruttle

As near as I can remember, this vessel's name was John Ruttle, a three masted vessel, about two hundred feet long, which had never taken passengers before. It had always been a freight vessel and was only fitted for this voyage to take passengers.

As steam had been but very little used up to this time, and the passenger fares on steamers were so much higher, most of the emigrants came in sailing vessels.

Never Again

Nowadays, no emigrant would dare think of ever coming in any other way than by steamer, where every modem elegance, comfort, and safety can be enjoyed. I think you could not induce one out of ten who have once crossed in one of those sailing vessels to attempt it again, even though they were allowed free passage. I don't know whether I could be induced to try it again if they should offer me a whole German city.

Cooking Onboard

First, there were no accommodations. Passengers received their provisions in the raw and were obliged to cook them themselves. The cooking places and vessels to cook in, were so limited that if you could cook a meal twice a day you would consider yourself very fortunate. This necessarily caused constant strife among the passengers, and some of the time they came to blows.

Water Shortage

The water supply was very limited so that we suffered for water, receiving only a limited amount of that most necessary article. The dire condition of it can only be imagined, when it was held in great, large, open tanks on deck subject to the sun and the rain. There was water all around, perhaps miles deep, and yet we suffered for water. As there were some showers of rain while we were on our voyage, we undertook to catch some in vessels. Alas, this was another sore disappointment, for when we tasted of it, it was bitter and salty like the ocean.

Our First Storm, Below Decks

On the third day out, when not quite out of sight of land, the deck steward came below and cautioned us to fasten our chests, trunks, and cooking utensils. Unfortunately, the warning was not well heeded, and some neglected to do this. In the night, the vessel began to pitch and toss, awakening the passengers out of sleep to find chests and tinware sliding from one side to the other, making a great racket.

It must be remembered again that we did not enjoy state rooms and berths like they have on the new ocean liners but were all in common on the lower deck below the hatches. Bunks were built up, one upon another, on either side of the hull, without any division of state rooms.

Here was one of the first "joys" of crossing the ocean in a sailing vessel. One can scarcely imagine the noise that occurred among the two hundred passengers of different nationalities and dialects. Some were screaming, some crying, some cursing, and some praying.

Some jumped out of their bunks, to catch a trunk or chest, and became jammed in between them, crying and yelling out for pain.

After a severe struggle with the storm, quiet was restored and baggage and utensils made fast and secure. For the balance of the voyage, though there were much rougher seas, this did not occur again. Most passengers took warning, but there were other experiences to come.

To continue reading this amazing true story, *The Joys and Sorrows of an Emigrant Family,* by Lt. Joseph Ruff, search for the title on Amazon.com or go to

www.MercerPublications.com

for details and a link.

To show your appreciation, please encourage the publisher by leaving a review on Amazon.com/Civil War Experiences of a German Emigrant. Thank you so very much.

Questions or comments: eMail: Dorothy@MercerPublications.com.

Photo Gallery

FARM HOME OF MR. JOSEPH RUFF, NEAR ALBION

Lot 68: Civil War CDV Card of Lieutenant Joseph Ruff of the 12th Michigan Infantry

The writing on the back. It looks like Joseph Ruff and Concord.

[Editor: Info: This CDV card was sold at auction in 2015 We would love to know where it is.]

Sold: $100
Bodnar's Auction Sales
July 30, 2015 4:00 PM EST
Edison, NJ, US
Reprinted by permission

Ruff Family Picture

Back Row: Lewis, Otis Kingsnorth, Lula Ruff Adams, Walter Dodes [editor: my grandfather], Millie Ruff Dodes, [my grandmother], Renny

Front Row: Viola Ruff Kingsnorth holding her two children Catherine and Stuart Kingsnorth, Joseph Ruff [my great-grandfather] Doris Dodes [Esther's sister] Catherine (wife of Joseph) [my great-grandmother] holding Esther Dodes [my mother] Rebecca Snyder

[Doris and Esther are children of Walter and Millie. Millie looks exactly like Esther did at that age. Doris and Millie were killed in an auto accident in 1935.]